AF382618

SUCCESSFUL JOB INTERVIEWS

Everything you need to win over recruiters

Written by Claude Matoux
Translated by Rebecca Neal

Coaching 50MINUTES.com

SUCCESSFUL JOB INTERVIEWS

- **Problem:** how can you win over a potential employer during a job interview?
- **Uses:** performing well during job interviews is a skill that can be learnt. Leaving things to chance will get you nowhere: in order to impress your interviewer, you need to prepare effectively.
- **Professional context:** job search, career change, request for a promotion.
- **FAQs:**
  - What should I say during a job interview?
  - Do I have to answer every question?
  - What should I wear?
  - Can I lie during an interview?
  - How should I talk about a negative experience?
  - How should I approach the interview if I have no professional experience, or if I am an older candidate?
  - How can I stand out from other candidates?

If your CV and cover letter have attracted a recruiter's attention, you have already cleared the first hurdle, but you are still one candidate among several: now it is up to you to prove to the interviewer that you are the right person for the job.

Very few people go into a job interview completely relaxed. Many candidates are scared that they will be judged harshly, that they will not be able to express themselves well enough and, more generally, that they will not be good enough. Given the feeling of failure and the financial consequences that accompany a rejection, especially now that jobs are in relatively short supply, these fears are far from unfounded.

What many people do not realise is that job interviews are stressful for the recruiter too. In the current economic climate, hiring someone new costs the company money, and it is in their best interests to pick the right person. A candidate who understands this will take care to constantly reassure the interviewer, inspire confidence in them and show them that they are the right fit for the role.

Lisa did not finish her studies and soon found an interesting job which she held for several years. However, she pushed herself too hard, developed health problems and was forced to give it up. One year later, her health has improved but she is scared that the fact that she does not have a degree will hold her back. Nonetheless, she has decided to go back to work and is practicing her interview skills: she gives thoughtful answers, speaks clearly and calmly and takes care of her appearance. In the space of a fortnight, she gets four interviews and is offered the job at the end of all of them. She now has the luxury of choosing the employer who is best for her, and opts for a chocolate company located near her house. Even though she is based in an economically depressed region, she has found a fulfilling job thanks to the effort she put into her interview skills, which made her shine as a candidate.

EFFECTIVE INTERVIEWS: THE BASICS

A job interview is a challenge and, provided that you really want the job, you have a lot at stake.

The recruiter starts evaluating you from the moment you arrive, and they will make a mental note of all the positive and negative points throughout the interview. Their list of positives will include everything likeable and reassuring about you, your skills and qualities, and your powers of persuasion. Their list of negatives will comprise all the times you hesitated, gave a poor answer or responded evasively. Watch out, because a single item in this list can put you out of the running, if it is something that the recruiter deems critical.

Contrary to popular belief, employers are not sadists who take pleasure in tormenting candidates by asking them trick questions. They just want to know who they are dealing with. In other words, they want to know who you are, what skills you have and how you react in given situations, and the only way to find out this information is to interview you.

Preparing for the most frequently asked questions will give you peace of mind as you approach your interview. It is better to think about the questions that the interviewer is likely to ask you than to hope that they will not ask you a particular question, as this obviously will not stop them from asking it. Even worse, you may end up so fixated on the question that you bring it up anyway even though the interviewer never asked you.

It goes without saying that it is the employer who leads the interview, as they are the one asking the questions. It is up to the candidate to give responses that are neither too short (as this forces the recruiter to ask follow-up questions and turns the interview into something of an interrogation) or too long (as the interviewer may lose interest partway through the answer). Structured responses make the candidate appear thoughtful and trustworthy. When an interview is going well, it is more like a conversation, with each person talking a similar amount.

"Tell me about yourself"

This question comes up in almost every interview and, although it is not meant to be a trap, it throws many candidates off balance, perhaps because they are not used to talking about themselves. Whatever the reason you struggle with this question, avoid simply telling the interviewer your name and reciting your CV, since you have already given them this information and they may even have it in front of them. One winning strategy is to explain how your professional trajectory relates to the position on offer, and to emphasise your motivations by talking about why you want to pursue this direction rather than any other.

"Why do you want to work for this company?"

Many candidates just want to earn a living (and there is nothing wrong with that!) and are not overly concerned about the company, as long as they have a job. The employer's point of view is completely different. They are not trying to hire someone for the sake of it: they want to find someone who has the right skills for the job and who they can count on.

If you want to give a good answer to this question, you must be well-informed about the company you are applying to. Look for information online, check out their offices before the interview or call them. Being unable to answer questions about the company will seriously dent your credibility, while doing your research and demonstrating your enthusiasm for the business will win you a lot of points. Your response to this question shows how passive or proactive you are.

"Why do you want to leave your current job?/Why were you let go from your last job?"

This question is more or less delicate depending on whether your contract ended as planned or you came into conflict with your employer. Keep your answer short and emphasise your interest in the job you are applying for now.

"Why do you want to work in this sector in particular?"

This question aims to test your motivation and check that your skills match up with what the employer is looking for. The interviewer is looking for someone who has thought carefully about their choice and is committed to their work. We all have our own preferences and talents, and since you are claiming that you are prepared to spend eight hours per day at this job, you should be able to explain why you have chosen this sector in particular.

"Why should we hire you?"

Or, why you rather than any other candidate? Even if the interviewer does not ask you this question directly, you can be sure that they are thinking it, so make sure that you give them an answer. It is not enough to say that you are the best candidate, as the employer only has your claim to go on and is unlikely to be convinced by it. You should show, not tell: the job requires particular experience, skills and qualities, and it is up to you to demonstrate that you have them. This is a delicate exercise, so practice is vital!

"What are your long-term goals?"

The answer to this question will differ depending on the job. In theory, it is good to be ambitious, as employers like candidates who know who they are and where they are going. However, make sure you do not take things too far – do not tell the person interviewing you that you want their job!

Unless you are just looking for a temporary job to pay the bills, in which case you should talk about your short- and medium-term goals, do not mention your plans to leave the company, especially if you have another project on the side.

"What is your greatest strength?/What are your three greatest strengths?"

This is the ideal question to sell yourself! Choose qualities that you possess and that are crucial for the role you are applying for. If you applied in response to a job posting, reread the job description and use it to prepare your answer.

Avoid mentioning qualities like punctuality, which do nothing to help you stand out from other candidates. Arriving late to work is bad, and getting there on time is a basic expectation. Furthermore, remember that if you claim to be "dynamic", "proactive" or "motivated", it is not enough to just say it; you also have to demonstrate this with your attitude.

EXTRA INFORMATION

Be specific when you talk about your qualities by giving examples from your experience and particular situations. For example, if you are applying for a role in accountancy, do not simply say "I am meticulous", but illustrate your claim with an example of a time when you did meticulous work and this helped your company. Similarly, if you want to work in the social services sector, instead of saying "I am a good listener", talk about a situation where your listening skills helped a person in difficulty.

- For example, a candidate can persuade the interviewer by saying: "I am very organised. I file all my documents as I go along, so my colleagues can find them straight away. I even arrange all the shirts in my wardrobe by colour".
- Another could say: "I am a good listener and communicator. During my internship, I dealt with an irate customer by letting them tell me about their situation and then explaining the reasons for their wait. They then apologised and even ordered from us again."

This approach makes your answers vastly more persuasive. Giving an example shows that you can really demonstrate these qualities, which is far more convincing than simply saying that you have them.

"What is your greatest weakness?/What are your three greatest weaknesses?"

This question is more delicate than the previous one. Mentioning a weakness that has nothing to do with the job you are applying for (for example, saying "I am greedy" when you are applying to work as an IT specialist) is completely useless for the interviewer. Nor can you mention weaknesses that will be worrying for the employer, such as "I am easily distracted" if you want to work in security, or "I am very talkative" if the role includes a confidentiality clause. The challenge is to highlight some areas where you could improve and stress the fact that you are working on them.

The STAR method is particularly useful here:

- Situation – describe a situation that you have experienced;
- Task – describe the work you had to do;
- Action – describe what you did;
- Result – describe the results you obtained.

- "I've always liked people, but I used to be very shy and I struggled to talk to them. I signed up for an improv class, and since then I've been more comfortable dealing with customers. I now enjoy persuading people, and last year I was given a bonus because my sales figures went up 7% from the year before."
- "I used to be too laid-back at work and I tended to put all my tasks off until the next day without really thinking about the consequences. I started looking into time management techniques and now I plan all my work."
- "I like being right, and I'm naturally stubborn. I know this is one of my weaknesses, so I've learnt to listen to other people and I'm now prepared to accept their views if they put forward good arguments. As a result, I enjoy teamwork much more now."

The STAR method can be used for any question that you can respond to by talking about a particular situation.

"What are your expectations in terms of salary?"

Do not tell them that salary does not matter to you or that you are prepared to accept whatever they offer you. Strangely, although many job seekers are looking for a position for a host of reasons, including (if not primarily) financial reasons, they generally only have a vague idea of what salary to ask for. Asking for the salary you want is part of being assertive, and not paying any attention to it makes you seem naïve.

If you cannot negotiate your salary, look for information online or through your trade union. If you can negotiate, do your research and always suggest a salary bracket to the employer in order to open a discussion. If you only put forward a single figure, you risk getting a flat refusal. Instead, show the employer that you are flexible and open to different possibilities.

"What are you looking for in a job?"

This question is about your values. Salary is far from the only criterion that influences your career and job choices. Our values, which we generally acquire very early on and which tend to change little over the course of our lives, drive us and shape our choices. From the employer's point of view, you will be more motivated and work more effectively if you agree with the company's values. Furthermore, you will feel far better if you get up every morning to do a job that you are well suited to as part of a team working on projects based on shared values. You have everything to gain by being honest. That said, you may want to stress different values depending on the company or sector you are applying to.

"What do you do in your free time?"

This is a friendly question. It allows the interviewer to find out about your interests, get a better idea of your personality and work out if you are more introverted or extroverted (if you will be working as part of a team).

Be cautious if you bring up any political or religious activities: these could be a great help or a great hindrance depending on whether or not the interviewer shares your affiliations.

Luck also plays a role in this question: if by chance

the employer shares one of your hobbies, this could play in your favour and make them more sympathetic to you.

"Do you have any questions?"

Your answer to this should always be yes! Questions are a sign of interest that should come naturally to you if you are really enthusiastic about the position. Do not ask (or at least do not open with) questions about the salary or other benefits, but rather ask for information about the company's current projects, the people you will be working with, any company-specific tools, and so on.

DELICATE QUESTIONS

Delicate questions are generally about gaps in your CV or health problems.

Employers do not like to see gaps in your CV: they are looking for someone who is active and trustworthy, and any breaks are liable to worry them. At the same time, they are still human beings, and they understand that finding a job is not easy and that people may have difficulties at one point or another in their lives. Honesty is therefore the best policy, as long as you do not play the victim.

Some candidates think that it is better to pursue education or training courses than to do nothing. Although this is generally true, you should watch out, because many employers do not see time spent in education or training as equivalent to time spent working. While it is a good thing to pursue further training and to indicate this on your CV, year and years of study may be counter-productive, because this is all time that you are off the job market.

Many employers will be understanding if you took time off work to raise your children, or if it took you a long time to find a job in a struggling sector, as long as you do not talk about it in a self-pitying tone.

Many candidates are unsure whether or not they should tell an employer that they have health problems. This choice has difference implications depending on the nature (physical or mental) of the illness, and particularly on whether you have successfully undergone treatment or are still suffering from it. If you are no longer unwell, you can present this in a positive light, though it should only be mentioned briefly. If you are still struggling with your illness, you need to think about yourself and your health: will you definitely be able to perform the job you are applying for?

Whatever your situation, be observant and adapt your behaviour based on that of the other person. While it is essential to prepare for an interview, you obviously cannot know in advance what questions you will be asked or what your interviewer's personality will be like.

THE INTERVIEWER

Interviewers may have different personality types:

- **Cold and distant.** They do not show any signs of friendliness, and may not even shake your hand. In general, candidates are afraid of this type of interviewer because they do not feel comfortable around them and do not receive the approval they are desperate for. Even so, do not draw any hasty conclusions: the interviewer may just be trying to stay objective, and in spite of their apparent frostiness, they may be inwardly impressed and offer you the job.

- **Friendly and welcoming.** This interviewer greets you with a big smile, does everything they can to put you at ease and may even confide in you. This is nice, but do not let it fool you. The interviewer may genuinely like you, or it could all be an act and they could have taken you out of the running early on, in spite of their apparent friendliness.
- **Strict and meticulous.** This type of interviewer is realistic, pragmatic and efficient. They calculate how much you are going to make and cost them. If your CV is not completely clear, they will take as long as they need to go through your career year by year.
- **Didactic and talkative.** They do not ask you many questions and spend a great deal of time explaining exactly what your work will be like if you accept the job. They listen carefully to your answers, and will often talk to you about their impression of you.
- **Multiple interviewers.** In some situations, you will not be responding to one person, but to a panel of interviewers with different

personalities. You will need to tread carefully, especially as there will be rapport and dialogue between the various people. The atmosphere may be relatively relaxed, or it could be more rigid (especially if there are procedures to respect).

Whatever your interviewer is like, say what you have to say, be polite and adapt your approach to the situation.

TOP TIPS

Although what you say is obviously vital, your behaviour is the deciding factor in your interview. This is where your interpersonal skills come into play. In theory, everyone who is applying for the job will be qualified for it (an applicant for a teaching position will have a degree in teaching, someone who is applying to be a mechanic will have studied mechanics, a candidate for a position as a doctor will have a medical degree, and so on). This means that the interviewer will differentiate between them based primarily on their behaviour, their motivation and their "aura"; in other words, on their nonverbal communication. Below are some key areas to focus on:

- **Your smile:** do not let the stress of the interview stop you from smiling! This is essential, at least at the beginning of the interview, because your smile draws other people to you. Do not wait until the end, because this will give the impression that you are relieved that it is over rather than happy to talk to your potential future employer. Studies have shown that we subconsciously associate smiling with intelligence, which means that you are likely to be seen as more intelligent if you smile than if you do not. Make sure your smile is natural, as a forced smile will have the opposite effect.

- **Eye contact:** look at the interviewer. Above all, do not lower your eyes or stare at the floor; even if you are just shy, this will make it look as though you want to get out of the situation.

- **Your gestures:** when you are talking, make little gestures to support what you are saying. You need to strike the right balance: gesticulating too much may be distracting, while not gesticulating enough will make you seem passive.
- **Distance:** norms regarding the amount of distance to maintain between people vary

depending on the culture. Do not invade your interviewer's personal space, but do not back away from them either. If there is a desk between you, put your hands on it to mark your territory. Hold a pen rather than fidgeting with your hands.

- **Your body position:** sit up straight. Hunching over or slouching indicates shyness or laziness, which are both turn-offs for employers. Stay relaxed: puffing out your chest is unlikely to make a good impression either.

- **Your voice:** the pitch and volume of your voice and the speed of your delivery have an impact on the general impression you give. While you have little control over the pitch of your voice, you can control the volume and your delivery speed (the more stressed a person is, the more quickly they speak). Practice speaking loudly enough, as it is difficult for your interviewer if they have to listen very closely to hear you, but do not overdo it or you may come across as aggressive.

- **Good manners:** obviously, politeness is important. Be courteous, avoid excessive familiarity, switch your phone off or put it on silent, shake your interviewer's hand if the opportunity arises, and thank them for their time at the end of the interview.

EXTRA INFORMATION

Make sure that your thoughts, words and behaviour are in tune with one another, as this will make you more convincing. If this is not the case, your interviewer will notice it or, at the very least, feel confused. If you say that you are motivated but drag your feet, sigh or yawn, nobody will believe you. On the other hand, if your face lights up when you talk about experiences that you are proud of, the interviewer will be won over.

FAQS

You never get a second chance at a first impression. Every time we meet someone new, we form an opinion about them, whether it is positive, negative or neutral, within the first few minutes. This is true for all situations, and is something to bear in mind during interviews: the first few minutes are decisive.

WHAT SHOULD I SAY DURING A JOB INTERVIEW?

Perhaps surprisingly, many candidates are unsure what to say. Obviously, the employer wants to know who the person in front of them is and what they can do, but talking about yourself is not always easy. This is why it is so important to know yourself well and to be able to set out your skills and qualities clearly.

The interviewer is the one who gets the ball rolling, but as the interview progresses, and especially if it is going well, you can also steer the conversation to an extent.

Talk about your skills and motivation for the position you are applying for. Avoid empty statements like "I want to thrive at your company". Your employer no doubt wants to see you thrive, but this is not their main motivation. Rather, they are interested in what you can offer them. Furthermore, "thrive" is somewhat vague and will mean different things to different people. Give concrete responses: who are you? What can you do? What do you like to do? Use examples drawn from your experience to support your answers.

In general, use positive wording in your answers. Say "I would be very happy to work for your customer service team" rather than "I wouldn't mind working for your customer service team". Can you see the difference?

Extra information

Your interviewer will probably have your CV in front of them during the interview. While there is nothing stopping you from getting someone to help you write it, you should be able to explain all the information on it. Not being able to clarify an aspect of your CV when asked will leave a very bad impression.

DO I HAVE TO ANSWER EVERY QUESTION?

Candidates know that they will have to answer a series of questions. But where is the line between your professional life and your private life? Can you refuse to answer some questions without effectively taking yourself out of the running?

If you refuse to answer a particular question, you may pique your interviewer's curiosity (what have you got to hide?). However, if you think that the question is too focused on your private life, you can say so while remaining calm. Even if the question strikes you as intrusive, do not respond aggressively, as this is always frowned upon. Be clear about what you are willing and unwilling to talk about; this is part of being assertive.

WHAT SHOULD I WEAR?

This question weighs on virtually every candidate's mind, and it is an important one, as your clothes will inevitably send your interviewer a message.

There is more than one "right" way of dressing for an interview, although there is one golden rule that applies to every situation: take your lead from the culture of the company you are applying to. Making an effort with your clothing is a way of showing respect. However, the most important thing is to be yourself rather than pretending to be someone you are not, so opt for clothes that you feel comfortable in. Companies rarely want you to look like a model (apart for some specific jobs where appearance is important), but all recruiters will want you to look clean and tidy.

EXTRA INFORMATION

Do not wear overly strong perfume or come to the interview smelling of cigarette smoke: these scents are often seen as unpleasant and will harm your image.

CAN I LIE DURING AN INTERVIEW?

Absolutely not! Having said that, you will need to be diplomatic, and there are always ways of putting a positive spin on the truth. It is better to keep quiet about any weaknesses, failures or past conflicts unless the interviewer brings them up. If they ask about them directly, briefly explain how you ended up in a particular situation without spending too long justifying yourself.

In particular, make sure you do not exaggerate your foreign language skills: a smart interviewer is likely to take the opportunity to ask you questions in the language you claim to know.

SOMETHING TO AVOID

Just because something is true does not mean you should bring it up in a job interview! For example, if a candidate in their forties is asked "What are your long-term goals?" and they respond by saying "I want to stay healthy until I can get my pension", this will obviously not win over the interviewer.

HOW SHOULD I TALK ABOUT A NEGATIVE EXPERIENCE?

Briefly. Employers also have life experience and know that there are some unscrupulous people out there. This means that they may be understanding about your situation, as long as you do not let yourself wallow in self-pity.

Failure is unavoidable in life, but winners' strength lies in their ability to bounce back. You can learn something from every negative experience, so focus on telling your interviewer about this, while making sure to accept your share of the responsibility. Blaming your failures on other people is irresponsible and never goes over well – few employers will want to hire someone who always plays the victim!

HOW SHOULD I APPROACH THE INTERVIEW IF I HAVE NO PROFESSIONAL EXPERIENCE, OR IF I AM AN OLDER CANDIDATE?

If you are just starting out in your career, emphasise your energy, interest in the job, flexibility and willingness to learn.

If you are older, draw attention to your experience, reliability and availability.

HOW CAN I STAND OUT FROM OTHER CANDIDATES?

This is the aim of the interview! Being a good or even a very good candidate is not enough: you need to show that you are motivated, and this should shine through in your words, actions and attitude.

Draw attention to the ways your personality is suited to the position you are applying for. To do this, you need to have a clear understanding of your strengths and be able to talk about them, and to research the company and the role.

Remember that the first few minutes are decisive: smile, make eye contact and give a good handshake. Express yourself clearly, without awkward pauses. It is important to show that you are comfortable; standing or sitting up straight and speaking in a clear, relaxed voice will help you to do this.

As soon as you arrive for your interview, you are being evaluated. Often, managers will ask receptionists, secretaries and the rest of the team for their input when selecting the right candidate. An important criterion is whether or not the others want to work with you. This means that you need to pay attention and be nice to everyone you encounter!

OVER TO YOU

1. ASSESS YOURSELF

Identify your knowledge (the theoretical understanding you have acquired), your know-how (your skills, the things that you know how to do in practice) and your social skills (your human and interpersonal skills). This will make it easier to talk to your interviewer about them. Emphasise the things that are specific to you and will enable you to stand out from the other candidates.

In addition, you should think carefully about the values that drive you and state them clearly. While everyone needs money to live, your salary is not the only thing that gets you out of bed in the morning. What are your values? These could include altruism, social recognition, diversity, independence, initiative, challenge, mobility, the enjoyment of being with other people, security, and respect for your private life, among others.

Do not skip this step: if you are not fully sure of who you are and what you can do, you will not be able to express this clearly during the interview.

Skills and values

Knowledge	
Know-how	
Social skills	
My values	

Remember that your personal, human and interpersonal qualities (soft skills in human resources parlance) are what will allow you to stand out from other candidates with the same profile on paper. Most companies pay just as much attention to soft skills as to hard skills (qualifications, abilities and experience).

Keep the following summary in mind:

2. PRACTICE IN FRONT OF A CAMERA

Use a camera or smartphone to record yourself answering the most frequently asked questions and watch the recording afterwards. This is the best way of seeing what you are already doing well and what you need to improve in order to win over your interviewer.

Do not be too hard on yourself: work on the weaknesses you notice without beating yourself up about them. At the same time, do not let yourself become complacent: instead of settling for good, strive for excellent. Remember that you are not the only person applying for the job, which is why preparation is so important. Analyse yourself objectively and put strategies in place to improve.

A FEW FINAL TIPS

- If you applied for the position in response to a job posting, analyse the job description closely so that you can base your arguments on it, and take it with you.
- Take any documents that could strengthen your candidacy with you: a letter of recommendation from a former employer, work that you have done, photographs, references from the internet, and so on. For example, if you are an artist,

take a portfolio of your work. Make every possible effort to show the interviewer what you can do.

- Minimise stress by practicing, arriving ten minutes early (leave yourself a buffer, because showing up late will create a bad first impression) and doing whatever helps you to relax (breathing exercises, listening to music, walking, and so on).
- Be assertive: tell the interviewer what you are looking for and do not be afraid to state your conditions. Candidates who grovel in front of the recruiter and say that they will accept anything do not end up getting the job. Employers prefer candidates who know what they want, who stand up for themselves and with whom they can negotiate realistic working conditions. Someone who knows what they want is reassuring to others.
- Finally, believe in yourself! Be yourself and give yourself time to think about the question you are being asked. If you are well prepared, it will not take you long to think of an answer. Think of the interviewer as someone who is interested in you and of

the interview as one good opportunity among many. It is a negotiation, so be professional, open and determined.

We want to hear from you!
Leave a comment on your online library
and share your favourite books on social media!

FURTHER READING

BIBLIOGRAPHY

- Bernardini, A. (1991) *Réussir un entretien d'embauche.* Paris: Marabout.

- Porot, D. and Bolles Haynes, F. (2008) *Best Answers to 202 Job Interview Questions: Expert Questions to Ace the Interview and Get the Job Offer.* Manassas, Virginia: Impact Publications.

- Ras, P. (2015) *Le grand livre d'entretien d'embauche.* Levallois-Perret: Studyrama.

ADDITIONAL SOURCES

- Lees, J. (2011) *The Interview Expert: How to Get the Job You Want.* London: Pearson.

- Reed, J. (2017) *Why You? 101 Interview Questions You'll Never Fear Again.* London: Penguin.

IMPROVE YOUR GENERAL KNOWLEDGE

IN A BLINK OF AN EYE !

www.50minutes.com